# The ABC's of Networking

Thom Singer

with Leslie Morris

## The ABC's of Networking
by Thom Singer with Leslie Morris

Published by:
New Year Publishing, LLC
144 Diablo Ranch Ct.
Danville, CA 94506 USA

orders@newyearpublishing.com
http://www.newyearpublishing.com

ISBN 978-0-9760095-2-8

*For my wife and my daughters:*
*Sara, Jackie and Kate.*
*You make my life complete.*


*For my three older brothers:*
*Steve Singer, Bill Singer and Bob Singer.*
*You have each contributed to my life and*
*I thank you for helping me become*
*the man I am today.*

## Acknowledgements

This book was not created in a vacuum. Many people have helped me in countless ways to complete this project. I appreciate all those in my personal and professional network who contributed with ideas, thoughts, advice, and moral support.

I would especially like to express my gratitude to Dave and Leslie Morris. Their entrepreneurial skills have made this book, and New Year Publishing, a reality.

Bob Phelan, my father-in-law, also deserves special thanks for donating his expertise of 40 years as a language teacher to helping me better craft the written word.

Thom Singer
Austin, Texas
March 1, 2007

# Contents

# ADDITIONAL CONSIDERATIONS

#  Attitude

There is no replacement for having a positive attitude.

Those who find the glass half full are always better off than those who complain. People like to associate with those who make them feel good, have an upbeat attitude and who search for solutions to problems.

Whiny people are just plain annoying.

A good example of this is comedian Bill Maher. Back when he hosted the Comedy Central television show, Politically Incorrect, he was thought to be the funniest guy on television. He had a great knack of lampooning everyone in Washington, and his own opinions stayed in the background. As this book is being written in 2007, his humor is based around how much he hates the President. He is not nearly as funny as he used to be because his jokes are cynical and mean-spirited.

Every workplace has its negative souls and you know exactly who they are. If you discovered the cure for cancer they would ask you, "But what about diabetes? You didn't cure that, did you?" These folks rarely have solutions, and often have better career opportunities pass them by because nobody wants to be dragged down by them. Then they proceed to blame others for their lack of advancement.

Better off are the people who have a positive attitude and seek out ways to improve the lives of those around them. Looking for the bright side and providing solutions will always serve you. Opportunities just seem to follow happy people around.

There are many things over which you have no influence ... but you can control your attitude, so have a positive one.

#  Brand

Coca-Cola® has a brand. Nike® has a brand. You have a brand.

It's true. In the Old West, cattle were branded so that they could instantly be identified to anyone who saw them roaming the prairies. The same is true of you. Everything you have ever done and said is part of your brand. Your past actions are an integral part of how others perceive you.

Similar to attitude, your image in the business community is very important to opportunities that will come your way.

Major corporations spend millions of dollars building and maintaining their brands. Many of us know people who make their livings as Brand Managers. They do this because there is quantifiable value in having a positive image to the outside world. Yet individuals often ignore the importance of managing their own brand.

You must always behave in a professional manner and pay special attention to how you act under stress. Here are two examples:

"John" is an accountant and is sure that his staff views him with admiration. His heart is in the right place, but when he gets overworked, he becomes irrational and downright ornery. He is branded as an awful person to work with. He has paid no attention to his brand and has allowed his reputation inside and outside his firm to become tarnished.

"Jeff" manages a team of financial services sales professionals. Jeff had spent years selling for the company before joining the management team and understands the difficulties that his direct reports can face on a daily basis. No matter what the situation, he remains calm and is quick to lend a hand. He tries to see all sides of a situation before responding and is fast to support those who work for him. Jeff is branded a team player.

Here are seven things you can do to improve your brand:

1. Treat others with respect

2. Volunteer for business and charitable organizations

3. Do a great job for your employer

4. Mentor others

5. Improve your public speaking skills

6. Write articles for business publications

7. Refer business to those in your network

Your behavior on a daily basis is what matters, not just how you perform on the job. Consistency is the key to developing a strong brand. The cliché, "Your actions speak so loudly that I could not hear what you were saying" is absolutely true in the establishment of your brand. People are watching you more often than you might think.

#  Creativity

Best-selling author Tom Peters said it best: You are either distinct or you are extinct![1]

If you want to stand out from your competition, creativity is a must. Too many people think that simply doing a good job is enough. These days, doing a good job is just the price of entry.

To be distinct, you need to look at what others in your industry are doing, and then do something different.

Several years back a regional law firm garnered national attention with their print advertising campaign featuring the managing partner's bulldog. It was so clever that people both inside and outside the legal industry knew about this firm and its not-so-cuddly mascot.

The competition's response? Dozens of law firms immediately began using animals in their media. One firm announced they wanted to do something different with their ads and did a campaign surrounding the managing partner's cat. How's that for taking copycat to a new level?

---

1  Tim Sanders, Love is the Killer AP. (Three Rivers Press, 2003)

Being a copycat will not generate attention for those who follow. Points for creativity are only awarded to those with fresh ideas. The law firms that subsequently ran advertisements featuring pets were seen as late to the party, and thus were ignored.

Creativity is not just limited to how you advertise, but instead applies to everything that you and your company do when interacting with the public. Look for new ways to entertain your clients in a manner they will always remember. One successful sales person who routinely brings clients to Broadway shows always mails the tickets to the client in advance of the show with a copy of the show's CD. Lots of sales people send tickets. How many add in the gift of music? Who will be remembered?

Make creativity a priority.

#  Determination

Determination is a key part of the equation in creating a strong network of professional contacts that can and will refer real business. To build true connections takes time and effort. If you think that networking just happens, you will be see lackluster results, if any at all.

The commitment to making, growing and keeping business relationships takes dedication along with determination. It is not something that you can only do on slow days. Networking is not part-time.

People often question why I still attend networking events after ten years of building contacts. They think I already know enough people. Yet I have not even begun to scratch the surface of building a successful network. It's a common misconception that once you build your brand you can slow down or even stop basic networking activities. Out of sight is out of mind.

Of course you must pace yourself to avoid burning out. Set aside one or two nights a week where you focus on networking. On the other nights spend time with your family, go out with your friends or go to the gym. Building your network is like running marathon, not sprinting to the finish line. Networks cannot be created overnight.

My friend Carol was a small business owner who was a champion at networking. She had become well known locally and nationally in her industry and she served on many committees and boards for various organizations. The more she networked, the more opportunities came her way. As commonly happens, she sold her very profitable business and pursued a long-time dream, fundraising for the arts. While Carol was nervous about making such a dramatic career change, she was confident that her extensive network of professional contacts would lead to success in her new field. And that was precisely what happened. Her major donors were cultivated from the network she had created in her old business. But she did not stop there; she continued to expand her network. She continues to recognize the power of relationships for her business today and for her uncharted future.

You have to focus to build a network. Be determined and stay determined.

#  Evangelist

In his book *The Human Fabric*, Bijoy Goswami tells us that there are just three personalities in the world: Mavens, Relaters and Evangelists. He explores the important characteristics of each type and then proclaims that the "Evangelists make things happen." He is right.[2]

Evangelists will tell anyone who will listen about what is important to them. They have the ability to persuade those around them to be believers. We want to follow them; we want to help them succeed. Evangelists are people with so much charisma and personality that people cannot help but to fall in line.

Goswami tells us that Evangelists have changed the world by believing deeply in a cause bigger than themselves. His examples include: Ronald Reagan, Steve Jobs, Martin Luther King, and General George Patton. Each of these men had a fierce passion which drove them to achieve great success. They inspired others to follow them and the results changed the future.

---

2   Bijoy Goswami, The Human Fabric. (Aviri Publishing, 2004) Page 53

If you want to make your world a better place, you must never slow down, never accept defeat and never stop believing. If you are serious about building a network, you cannot be shy. Be an Evangelist and create a band of followers who will help realize your dreams.

#  Follow Up

When you exchange business cards with someone, they are not automatically part of your network. It's easy to confuse knowing someone with actually being in someone's network.

Building a business relationship requires a series of interactions. You need to understand their business and who would be their ideal clients. They need to know the same thing about you. Too often people meet a new business contact and add them to their database, neglecting to think about the next steps.

Networking is all in the follow up.

If you have a conversation with someone at a business function, the best thing to do is to follow up a few days later with an email, phone call or handwritten note. This gesture is a way to remind the other person of you, and allows you to take the next step of having lunch or inviting them to attend another business event.

Keep in mind that to have someone become a valuable part of your network, you need to have seven to ten personal interactions. Anything less than that makes them just a person you know. By proactively following up, you will move them into your network at a faster pace. If you wait for the other person to contact you, you may wait for a long time.

Since it is the follow up that makes the relationship, paying attention to the types of follow up is important. Sitting down and having a meal with someone, or playing a round of golf is always better than just seeing them around town at subsequent networking events. However, such encounters take planning and timing. You need to make sure that the other person is also looking to advance the relationship.

In many ways, building a business relationship is similar to dating. The first day someone meets a potential mate they do not propose marriage. Instead, they look for different opportunities to see the other person again, and slowly build on shared experiences. The same is true in networking. It's a good strategy to start with shorter encounters. Meeting for coffee or lunch is much less of a time commitment than a round of golf or dinner with your spouses.

Make following up with people a priority on your daily schedule.

#  Game Plan

Professionals often execute on their networking, marketing, business development, public relations, and branding without having a game plan.

If you want to achieve results, you have to know what success looks like. You cannot measure the outcome if you do not know in advance what you are trying to accomplish. This requires taking the time to create a plan and then reverse engineering the steps involved in getting you there.

Tim Hayden, the CEO of an experiential marketing firm, understands the importance of knowing what success looks like for his clients. According to Tim, it is all about knowing in advance what actions a company or individual needs to take to get noticed over all the "noise" in the marketplace.

From Tim's web site:
*GamePlan Marketing & Events is an experiential marketing agency that creates and executes strategies where brands achieve positive, measurable results through integrated marketing practices and events. Respecting the*

*unique challenges set before each of our clients, we build*
*winning campaigns and events that generate demand, gain*
*exposure and create awareness.*

Tim and his team will only work with clients who can
clearly articulate what they are trying to accomplish.
While many companies create events, parties and other
"over the top" experiences, many do not take the time to
figure out what constitutes successful marketing. This can
leave them with big expenses and little tangible results.

Creating a game plan requires committing the plan to
writing. Too often, executives will give lip service to an
idea, but do not make the investment in thinking it thor-
oughly through. There is something magical about having
your game plan printed and tangible. It makes the ideas
and next-steps easier to accomplish when you have them
in front of you.

Does your company know how to define success? Do
you? Do you have a game plan to lead you toward a
dominant position in your industry?

If not, get going on your game plan.

#  Help

If you want other people to assist you in your career, you first must find ways to help them. Very often people will make a commitment to networking, and after a few months sour on the whole process. When asked why networking is not working for them, they will reply with "the people I have met do not refer business."

If you think that meeting business professionals and handing them your business card will make them run back to their desk, dive into their database, and spend hours telling the world about you and your company, you are not just wrong, you are delusional.

To really inspire others to become a referral source, you need to find ways to help them with their business first. Most people will try to return the favors.

Take an hour each week to go through your contacts and look to see how you can be of value to others. Review the names of people in your network and think of whom you can introduce them to, or other ways that you can help them.

Here are some ideas:

1. Do you know a local reporter for your local business journal (or other publication) with whom you can have lunch? While at lunch, share with them positive and colorful stories about local business people. This is a double win; reporters love to meet interesting people in the community because one never knows what stories they will be assigned in the future, and it helps those in your network, as maybe the reporter will want to feature their business in a story!

2. If you are going to be attending an interesting business event, forward the information to others who would benefit from attending. Better yet, invite them to come as your guest.

3. Plan a breakfast or happy hour at a local gathering place and invite the key members of your network. My friend Scott has put together a group called the Get It Group (those who "get" how networking really works) which meets once a week. The participants look for ways to help each other and everyone appreciates Scott's efforts in arranging the meeting.

If you look for ways to help others you will see results. Plus, it just feels good to be of assistance to someone else.

#  Intensity

> *"Ultimately, it is your career, and you must take charge of it. Create value, capitalize on opportunity, and always let the world know how great you are!"*[3]
>
> David Lorenzo

His book, *Career Intensity: Business Strategy for Workplace Warriors and Entrepreneurs*, has loads of advice for anyone who wants to take their career to the next level. This is not a job hunter's guide, but rather a success manual for anyone who is looking to advance his or her career.

The intensity Lorenzo encourages us all to embrace is the very same spark that we see in peak performers. One common thread in successful entrepreneurs and top executives is the drive for continuous individual improvement. This is not a genetic trait; it is a focused strategy. Intense attention to what you want to accomplish is a competitive advantage in today's individual economy.

---

3   David Lorenzo, Career Intensity: Business Strategy for Workplace Warriors and Entrepreneurs. (Ogman Press, 2006) Page 194

Regardless of your goals, success does not happen by accident. You need to tackle the little things every day to reach
your goals. To do anything less will leave you unfulfilled.

Do you know in your heart that you can do more with
your life? Can you be one of the great ones in your industry? Do something about it.

Take charge. Focus. Plan. Network. Create value. Engage
your intensity.

#  Journey

Your career is not just about getting to some ending point. Too often I find myself looking toward goals and I forget to enjoy the milestones along the way.

A 50-year-old man approached me after I spoke at a conference. He was concerned with my assertion that those who develop the best networks and get referrals and other huge business opportunities spend up to 10 years cultivating relationships.

He said, "I have five decades behind me. Five decades in which I have never focused on networking. Now I am learning it is imperative to have strong business contacts. But if what you say is true, then it will be as many as ten years before I see the benefits?" I told him that in ten years he will be 60 whether he builds a network or not!

His concern was with the end result, not with the advantages he will have along the way. The payoff is not just about achieving the end result of having a large network, it is about the experiences you will have with the people you meet each and every day.

While it might take him ten years to grow his network to
a grand scale, along the way he will make many valuable
connections. Some results will happen immediately, others
will take more time. An accountant I know told me that
he called on one of his clients regularly for 18 years
before finally turning the prospect into a client. However,
during this time he also developed a great friendship
with the prospect.

Keep your destination in mind while enjoying the journey.

#  Knowledge

Do you believe in the cliché "Knowledge is Power"?

To be successful in your business community and industry, you need to have knowledge. You want to be seen as the Go To Person. While doing a good job in your specific role is important, only mastering one topic will get you passed over for a variety of opportunities.

Consider what interests you. Have a broad range of topics that you learn about outside of your area of expertise. You should read newspapers, magazines, trade journals, blogs, websites, and books on a variety of topics.

Are you thinking, "it takes a lot of time to read that much"? Yes, it does. No one said that any of this came easily! Carve out an hour every day and dedicate this time to increasing your knowledge. Leave for work a little early and stop at a coffee shop to read the paper if you cannot find the time to do so at home or the office. One of my friends has a daughter in elementary school and he makes a point to read with her every night. He reads the weekly news magazines and she reads her chapter books.

Leaders are readers. Successful executives read and study multiple subjects. They have a natural curiosity about the world and can converse with people from any part of the world, religion, political affiliation, industry, etc.

If you are not doing enough to learn something new every day, do something about it. There are no barriers to finding ways to gain knowledge.

#  Leading Edge

According to the American Heritage Dictionary, *Leading Edge* is defined as:

*1. The edge of a sail that faces the wind. 2. The front edge of an airplane propeller blade or wing. 3.a. the foremost position of a trend or movement. b. Someone or something occupying such a position.*[4]

Are you on the leading edge in your company, industry or business community? Does your competition pay attention to your every move? Or do you just follow the leader?

If you want to build a strong reputation in your field you need to be a pioneer. Being the same as everyone else in your industry is mediocre and those who are average rarely finish on top. You must look for ways to stand out from the crowd and deliver increased value to all that you encounter.

- Within your company you need to be the thought-leader on a variety of topics.

---

4 American Heritage Dictionary of the English Language, Third Edition. (Houghton Mifflin Company, 1992) Page 1023

- With your clients you need to be seen as highly capable and dedicated to being a partner in their success.

- With your network you need to be seen as a person who gladly helps others and looks for ways to make connections.

You do not get to the leading edge by accident. To be an industry leader you have to be focused on excellence and be able to communicate your unique skills to everyone you encounter. You cannot by shy or afraid to take charge of the situations at hand.

Be confident when in front and others will follow. Or you can allow your competition be the leading edge. Your choice.

#  Mega

If you want to succeed with networking or anything else in your life you need to:

Go Big or Go Home!

Many people try to achieve success without having a BHAG (Big, Hairy, Audacious Goal). Do you think that Henry Ford began with visions of a little car company? Did Michael Dell revolutionize the computer industry with small goals? Did Walt Disney succeed by just wanting to make mouse cartoons?

No. All of these companies achieved greatness because they sought industry domination. Their founders had MEGA goals that others laughed at for their loftiness. They did not settle for small.

Do not just host events, host **amazing** events. Don't just treat people well, treat them like **gold**. It is not just about delivering average products and services, deliver the **best** products and services. And don't just set goals, set MEGA goals.

Mega success is a product of mega goals.

While unsuccessfully Googling to find who first coined the phrase "Go Big or Go Home", I discovered a book by the same title by Wil Schroter. Schroter is an author, speaker, consultant and syndicate columnist. He had some great points about mega thinking on his blog:

**Vision** – Think BIG, the way Google, PayPal and Skype do.

**Growth** – Learn how to compress time to grow faster than your competition.

**Marketing** – Position your company as Number One right from Day One.

**Capital** – Forget raising capital, learn how to create capital and leverage what you have today.

**Management** – Leverage your smaller size to run circles around your larger competitors.

This is great advice for anyone in search of success. Even if you do not reach your target, by setting mega-huge-giant goals you are more likely to outpace your competition. Being average will get you results, but not the mega huge rewards that you are seeking.

#  Name Recognition

A lawyer proudly told me that his firm was "the best kept secret in the legal industry." He felt that marketing and advertising would "cheapen" his professional standing. Unfortunately, the poor guy was just leaving money on the table.

There is nothing wrong with touting your own successes. In fact, if you don't do it, no one else will. While you should not be braggadocious, you have to take responsibility for letting others know who you are and what you do. People do business with people they know and like. If they do not know you, they will take their dollars to your competition.

Having name recognition in your business community means that others will help you reach your goals. They can become your best assets by singing your praises to others, in effect becoming your virtual sales team.

There are many ways to achieve name recognition. But a combination of the following can be very effective: writing articles, giving speeches, volunteering your time for charity, authoring a book, being interviewed by the press, advertising, networking, attending industry trade shows, and creating a newsletter or blog.

Name recognition does not happen by accident. It takes effort. And once you achieve a level of fame, there will be jealous people who talk negatively about you. But if you have good character and treat people fairly, the naysayers will be few and far between.

Opportunities find their way to those who are known. There are always people who say things such as, "WOW, Mark is so *lucky* to have gotten that job" or "Sally is an *overnight* success!" It is not luck and it did not happen overnight. It is that these people have built a solid reputation.

Some years ago my father-in-law was admiring a painting and asked the artist how long it had taken her to do the work. She answered "twenty years and three weeks." The painting itself had taken three weeks, but twenty years of experience prefaced those three weeks.

How about you? You should be a known quality brand in your business, not the best kept secret. There are potential clients who could benefit from knowing you and your business. You owe it to them to let them know you exist. Starting today will get you there much faster than simply waiting around to begin some time in the future.

#  Others

When you are building a network of professional contacts that can and will refer you business, you must remember the golden rule:

*Do unto others as you would have them do to you.*

And then do more for them.

Quite often people believe when they meet people in a networking setting, that these new acquaintances will immediately start sending them referrals. Without having built a true business friendship, people wait for the phone to ring. If new business does not roll in, they lose faith in the whole process.

Meanwhile, they do nothing to help the other people.

While we are all hoping that our networking efforts will lead to increased business opportunities, you have to remember that other people are hoping for the same results. By actively looking for ways to serve others, you will be more successful.

Does that mean that everyone you help will instantly find ways to send you business? No. Some may not have the ability or connections that will benefit you. Others are selfish and never help others. It is not about keeping score, but instead it is about positioning yourself as a resource.

I always try to find out whom others want to meet in the local business community. When I see the opportunity to make an introduction, I will follow up with an email or a phone call introducing the two people. While I get nothing directly from their interaction, by making the effort to help others in my network, I know that others will do the same thing for me in the future.

Steve Harper describes this in his book *The Ripple Effect*. Harper says that if you toss a rock into a pond, the ripples will go out and affect the whole body of water. At some point the ripples will hit the sides and return to the center.[5] This is absolutely true in networking.

Discover ways to help others without expectations. Your efforts to be a resource will make you more than just another business person, but rather you become an important advisor to those in your network.

---

5   Steve Harper, The Ripple Effect. (SWOT Publishing, 2005) Page 23

#  Persistence

*"Nothing in the world can take the place of persistence. Talent will not; nothing is more common than unsuccessful men with talent. Genius will not; unrewarded genius is almost a proverb. Education will not; the world is full of educated derelicts. Persistence and determination alone are omnipotent. The slogan 'Press on' has solved and always will solve the problems of the human race."*

Calvin Coolidge

I often witness people give up on their business goals. They start the year with conviction, and plan their resolutions. New Year Resolutions are a good idea; most people plan to work harder, start a business, expand their network, write articles for their industry trade journal, etc. However by mid-year most are stuck in the routine of mediocrity and have stopped thinking about achieving greatness. Having that resolution is part of the equation, but having the persistence to keep working toward that goal is what makes the difference.

When I began to write my first book, *Some Assembly Required*, I thought it would take about six months. Instead it took more than 18 months. My editor and I kept moving the project forward even when we were both overwhelmed with other priorities in our lives. Sure, there were missed deadlines, but we were committed to the book. We were not "lucky" to have had the time to write a book, we were persistent.

Have you ever watched "extreme sports" on TV? These skaters, skiers, skydivers, bikers and mountain climbers are amazingly talented. However, they were not born with these skills. It took years of practice to learn how to do the death-defying moves. It took guts. It took crazy bravery. They did not give up along the way. The same is true for those who are the peak performers in the business world.

You will achieve some of your goals and not others. The difference is always persistence.

# Questions

Asking questions is an important part of networking and business development. Many of us like to talk, but knowing what your clients and prospects want to hear is even more important. My dear dad once told me, "You have two ears and one mouth – use them accordingly."

While listening twice as much as you talk is easy in theory, it is harder to execute. This is especially hard if you make your living in sales. It is a natural tendency to want to share the benefits of your products or services with anyone who will listen. I love to tell stories. But I have found when I ask others about what is important to them, I gain valuable information that helps me better serve them in the future.

By finding ways to solve problems, you will become a resource. And a resource always wins over some random sales guy!

Here are eight questions that are appropriate to ask of people you meet in business settings:

1. What is your biggest challenge this year?

2. Who is your ideal client or prospect?

3. What could happen that would make this month incredibly successful?

4. What are your goals this year?

5. Where would you like to see your career/business in five years?

6. In a perfect world what could your (insert your industry: banker, lawyer, accountant, etc.) be doing for you?

7. Who in your business community would you most like to meet?

8. What can I do to assist you?

The answers to these questions will help you discover ways to add value to anyone you meet. Once you know what others need, look for ways to solve their problems. By doing this, you will become more valuable to those in your network.

If you do not ask others what they need, you will never know how to provide it.

#  Respect

That you need to *treat* others respectfully should go without saying.

Go beyond this, however, and consider how you *think* about people. Which of their characteristics do you focus on?

Too often we focus in on someone's shortcomings. It makes us feel more successful to ponder areas where they fail. If all you see is someone's faults, how can you really admire them or work with them? Without admiration, can you really show them respect?

When I look at my calendar each morning I review the list of people whom I will encounter during my day. These people include co-workers, clients, prospects, referral sources and family members. I then think of two things I admire about each person. By spending the time to look for positive traits, it makes my interactions with others much more enjoyable.

Yes, sometimes you have to deal with difficult people and ones you don't even like, but if you look hard enough you can find something good in nearly everyone. When your mind is in tune with the positive traits in others, your

conversations will be more pleasant. You do not even
need to tell them about what you admire, even though it's
nice to do so should you feel the urge. If you are conscious
of your respect for the other person, they will know it.

Make a point to know what makes people special. Then
treat them as the spectacular person that they are.

#  Sincerity

When building a professional network that will assist you in growing your career, you must have the right motivation. You should genuinely look to connect with others in your business community with whom you can create mutually beneficial relationships.

If your motive is just to find people who will send you referrals, and you do not plan on putting in the work to help others, you won't be successful. Notice that in the middle of the word "networking" is the word *work*. Do the work. If you do not assist others, over time you will be seen as a taker. Those who are selfish with their intentions should stay home.

My college roommate's father had this down. For many years he owned and ran a successful collection agency, where he was the biggest asset – the source of business development. Anywhere he went, he talked to people. This was not because he was overtly looking for new clients. In fact, his agency's niche was quite specialized. It was simply because he was genuinely interested in people. As a bonus, it served him well in business.

Tips to remember about being sincere:

- If you meet someone who is influential but you do not like them, do not invest the time to build a relationship with them. It would not be sincere to build a friendship just because they have connections. That would be manipulation.

- If someone in your network is helping you, look for ways to be return the favor. If you do not clearly see a way to benefit them, ask what you can do to be of assistance. But you have to sincerely mean it, and then follow through.

- Be polite to everyone with whom you interact. There is a fine line between showing genuine interest in people and kissing up to people to gain their friendship. Be yourself, your nicest self, but not phony.

Nothing proves your sincerity more than longevity. Many people will come and go in the business world. Those who last two, three, ten years on top will have their secrets exposed; that is why you should always be sincere. Anything less will eventually be known to all.

#  Tenacity

If you want to succeed in business, you can never quit. There are countless examples of successful people who routinely faced major obstacles along their path to greatness. They did not roll over and play dead. They did not quit. Successful people are tenacious.

It is well known that Abraham Lincoln lost many elections for lower office before winning the presidency. And let's not forget that Thomas Edison conducted more than 10,000 different experiments before his breakthrough invention of the electric light bulb.

It is said that the average sales person gives up on a prospect after he or she has attempted to reach them five times. Yet it is also said that the average person does not call a vendor back until they have received seven phone calls. That means that the tenacious sales person will get more appointments (and thus sales) than the average sales professional.

Networking can be very complicated. Most people think networking is just going to after-hours events, having a few drinks and waiting for the referrals to roll in. This is why so many people give up on networking. When they do not see immediate results, they abandon the whole concept.

To achieve real results with your networking means that you have to be tenacious. Many people you meet will be great connections for you; however, it takes a long time to build meaningful relationships. Stick with it. Find ways to make building your network part of your daily routine.

Visualize your goal for having productive networking relationships and then go for it. Do not let anyone or anything stand in your way.

#  Urgency

The best time to build your network is now. Do not procrastinate, as you never know when you will need the assistance of others. But remember that not everyone will share your sense of urgency, thus you have to work hard to create connections, but respect the other person's desire to move the friendship forward at their own pace. Networking with many people at one time allows you to respect the natural pace of expanding relationships, and be sure there's always someone with whom to have coffee or lunch. Keep your networking pipeline as full as your business development pipeline.

As you focus your attention on building a network of professional contacts, you will have the opportunity to meet many fascinating people. It is important that you plan for follow up with those whom you meet, and that you do so in a timely manner. Timing is urgent.

Creating a real network is not done at networking events. These events are just a tool to put business professionals in the same room. Real connections are made in the follow up. To establish a network involves multiple points of contact between you and others. Much like when you are dating, the first meeting did not establish the romantic relationship. That part came later with the discovery of mutual interests and shared experiences.

Too often we meet others and do nothing to initiate the next step until it is too late. Have you ever run across the business card of someone you met months ago and thought, "Argh. I never followed up with them"? It happens all the time. People wait to make contact and then the opportunity is gone.

Be prompt in your follow up. There is a real urgency for you to strategize on just how you will make contact with new contacts. An email, handwritten note, or a phone call cannot wait for more than three days, or you will be a distant memory.

I prefer sending a handwritten note, and I make the time to do them every Wednesday and Friday. I mail notes to anyone that I have met in the previous few days whom I would like to get to know better. I do this not just to people I meet networking, but also any prospective client that I might have called on for the first time. Very few people send handwritten notes, so the effort is noticed.

Treat all aspects of networking with urgency and you will see better results.

#  Vision

Whom do you want as part of your professional business network, and how do you expect your network to be of assistance? Those who are successful in their networking efforts do not just expect to meet people and then await results. Successful people are visionary, and not just in business.

If you are on a plane flight from Los Angeles to Honolulu, you would want the pilot to know where he or she is going and to visualize that success is a safe landing at the Honolulu Airport. If not, they would just be taking off and flying west. If you look at a map, there is a lot of ocean out to the west of California. To just hope that the plane would land on the runway is a big gamble. Your pilot needs to clearly see where he or she is going. The same is true for anything you want to achieve in your career.

Take a long, hard look at whom you currently network with and examine if the people you know are in the industries you desire to do more business with. See if the individuals have the status and the commitment to be a mutually beneficial resource. While knowing a lot of hip or interesting people is nice, it is more important that you recognize if you know the right type of business people. Some will not have the cachet to open doors for you. Others will not choose to do so. If you have holes in your network, you need to identify them and then make a plan to add people to your circle of influence who have the connections you need.

Now take the time to sketch out the industries you do business with, and write down the names of the people you know who work in or around these types of prospective clients. This will help you see where the strengths in your network are, and where you have weaknesses. Additionally, actually putting this on paper will make it tangible. You will be able to see exactly where your networking efforts need to be focused.

Know what success looks like (Steven Covey says "begin with the end in mind") and see it clearly in your mind. Have a vision of what you want and how to get there. Know who can help you along the way. Then go do it.

#  Wisdom

*"One cannot have wisdom without living life."*
Dorothy McCall

*"It is a characteristic of wisdom not to do desperate things."*

Henry David Thoreau

Wisdom is more than knowledge, it is to objectively understand what you have learned and act accordingly. Entire books have been written on the subject of wisdom, but essentially it comes down to good judgment and common sense.

When we are young, our enthusiasm and passion sometimes take control of our actions. This can lead to some regretful circumstances. Most look back at youthful indiscretions where they acted or spoke in the heat of the moment and know they would respond differently in the present. While their position might have been correct, they ruined a relationship, friendship or their reputation because of their impetuous actions.

One of my favorite sayings is *"Youth is wasted on the young."* While I look back on the endless energy that filled my life back in those days, much of it was misdirected or totally unfocused. I would love to have that gumption I had at 22. And if I did, I would be able to move mountains. Yet I would not be where I am today without the trials, tribulations, bad choices and missteps that I took along the way. It has been the sum of those experiences that makes us understand the relationship between wisdom, maturity and age.

Embrace wisdom, both your own and that of others in your network. The experiences of others can be as valuable to your own education as that of your own. That is why you should seek out and find a mentor who has lived the life you desire. While finding someone to be your mentor is not always easy, when you have a trusted advisor, your path to success can be much easier.

Conversely, not everyone becomes wise as the years go past. Learn to recognize those who have not learned from their experiences, good and bad. Many allow their ego to cloud their judgments and never get past themselves. The best action is to avoid these individuals.

Those who have real wisdom naturally give back to others in their community and so should you. It is not enough to have just existed. To be successful you must understand the "why" behind your experiences. This is wisdom.

# XYZ is the End

What? There is no end to networking. Get back out there!

This is not a joke. There really is no end to your efforts to make, grow and keep your business relationships. While building and cultivating relationships with people takes a lot of work, if you neglect to make it a priority, then your network will wither away. Continue to nurture your existing business friendships and remain open to welcoming new people into your life. Those who have learned "The ABC's of Networking" know that it is not something to wish for, but rather it is about making personal human relationships part of their lifestyle.

*Have Fun!*

# ADDITIONAL
# CONSIDERATIONS

# Party Time!

Hosting a reception for your clients, prospects and "friends of the firm" can be one of your best business development tools if done correctly. If done wrong, it is a waste of time and money.

The good news is that it can be done easily and without having to spend tons of cash. This is not to imply that it will be cheap; a quality event will involve a financial commitment. However, this investment, depending on the number of attendees, will be no more expensive than running an advertisement in a business publication.

The bad news is that most firms make poor spending decisions that cause them to spend too much money and fail to bring out their targeted guests.

Here are five tips to help you make your next client event a success:

1. **Target your local business contacts.** Regardless of how many national clients you have, very few people will travel to attend a party, unless you hold it in conjunction with some other type of user meeting or educational seminar (which is a great thing to do, by the way). While extending an invitation to out-of-towners is a nice courtesy, unless they have

another reason to be in the area, don't expect them to show up. Keep this in mind when planning how many guests you will actually have in attendance.

2. **Selecting the venue and day of the week.** Where you hold your event has a lot to do with the success of the event. If you are fortunate enough to have a large reception area or nice patio at your place of business, hold the party in your own space (caveat: as long as you are centrally located to your local business community). It can help keep your costs down since many hotels and restaurants charge higher rates than a caterer, especially for alcohol. Shop around for a caterer; you do not *need* the highest priced catering company in your town. As long as the food is of good quality, no one will notice.

In addition to the cost savings, having people visit your place of business helps build a closer bond with them. Clients and others like to see your facility and this gives you a chance to show off your technological and other competitive advantages.

If you do not have an office that can accommodate a large group, try renting a whole restaurant for a couple of hours. If your party is scheduled early (before their dinner rush), many restaurants will gladly give you part or all of their space if you are expecting enough people. The right bistro can have a much nicer feel than a hotel or country club ballroom. Also look to museums or other unique venues.

Try doing a business cocktail party on a Tuesday or Wednesday evening from 5:30 p.m. - 7:30 p.m. Mondays are too hectic, and the weekend is family time for many people. Everyone will have an opinion on what day of the week is best, but you want a day that is not going to compete with lots of other events. Don't make your guests choose; hold your event on a "free" night. Also, hosting it at an early hour will allow people with young children to come to your event and still make it home in time to tuck them into bed.

3. **Your Guest List.** This is an area where many professional service firms short change their party before it even gets started. They limit their list to only clients or other VIPs, and then their short list does not produce enough live bodies to have a good party. While you do not want to invite everyone in town, you need to invite three to four times your targeted attendee number. Include anyone at a client company with whom you interact. In addition, invite executives from other companies that serve

your clients (not your competition). If you are a law firm, be sure to invite the partners from all the local accounting firms, consultancies, venture capitalists, bankers, etc. These people are commonly referred to as "friends of the firm", as they are not your clients or prospects, but they are your friends. They will also be cherished advisors to many of your party guests, and building relationships with these professionals is vital to your own success.

Do not rely on your invitation alone to attract your attendees. It is the responsibility of everyone in your company to follow up with their contacts by telephone to personally invite them to the party. This is a great chance to connect with them and it makes sure that the person got the invitation (spam filters and secretaries often stop invites from reaching the executive). In addition, if they personally tell you they will come, they are more likely to actually show up.

4. **Speeches and other pontifications.** Avoid them whenever possible. Unless the event is a grand opening or company anniversary, do not let your senior executives get up and make long speeches. Too often these talks are ignored as the guests continue to mingle and talk over the person making the announcement. This is embarrassing for the speaker

and the audience. If you do manage to quiet everyone to total silence, you have successfully killed the momentum of the networking that was taking place. Following the speech, many guests will make this the opportunity to leave the party.

If a presentation is necessary, make sure that it is brief. This is not the time to recognize everyone in your company or show a long video that is really just a commercial for your firm. Make the party about the party. Let your guests have fun. When they interact with other VIPs and make valuable business contacts, you win.

5. **Name Tags.** Always have name tags for business events. Some executives do not like name tags, and will discourage their use. But name tags are an important tool to facilitate networking. While you may know all the guests, they do not necessarily know each other. You will want to pre-print the name tags to avoid causing a back up at the door. Be sure to put their first and last name *and* the company name on the name tag, and make sure the font is as large as possible. You want people to be able to read the name and company from a distance. And do not forget to have plenty of blank name tags and a Sharpie® available for those impromptu attendees.

# Cough on Everyone

The last several years have proven the effectiveness of viral marketing. But viral marketing, word of mouth advertising and networking do not just happen. Everyone in your company must be proactive and reach out to clients, prospects and others VIPs.

However, too often business people think others will do the work for them. Executives think that the tasks of promoting the company belong only to the sales and marketing organizations. Sales people expect marketing to magically make the phone ring, while marketing professionals await direction from the management or sales teams. It is a never-ending cycle of passing the buck and pointing fingers.

Most companies could produce better results if everyone started coughing all over everyone. Just as the flu, or any virus, is spread through human contact, awareness about your firm requires you to be talking with people. Your team needs to be having constant contact with the business community. If there is no contact, they don't get sick. The same is true of your clients and prospects; if you are not consistently giving them your message, then they are not going to be moved to do business with your company.

# Do it Anyway

No matter how much we enjoy the various aspects of our personal and professional lives, some days we just don't want to get out of bed.

You know the feeling when you hit the snooze button for the fifth time. The thought of taking a shower and driving to work makes a root canal sound appealing. And the last thing you want to do is happily engage in conversation with co-workers, clients, prospects or any other human. We all have those days.

While playing hooky might make us feel better in the short term, it won't let us accomplish anything for the day, which will just leave us feeling worse tomorrow.

This is especially true if part of your job function involves business development. When you are not feeling on top of your game, it is easy to push these more outgoing aspects of your job to a lower level of priority. You often see this with accountants, lawyers and other professional service firms. They know they should be networking and looking for future business, but they just don't feel up to it, so they hide under the covers of the current client work, repetitively hitting the proverbial "snooze button."

But without cultivating tomorrow's business today, we could find ourselves without anything to do tomorrow. So do it anyway. Pick up the phone and schedule a lunch meeting or take a client to happy hour. Action will lead to results.

# Network Everywhere:

## A Thom Singer Story

The day after Christmas 2006 I decided to brave the local shopping mall. My wife and I had gone to lunch, and I mentioned that I needed some new clothes for work, thinking that the Nordstrom Men's Sale might have some good deals. She dropped me off at the mall so that I would not have to hunt for parking, and propelling me into "shopping hell," promised to return three hours later.

I had never been to the mall the day after Christmas and had no idea what I was really in for. Once I entered the mall I decided to grab a cup of coffee to perk me up before my sale rack adventure, but the line at the coffee bar was about 20 people deep. My patience was already short, and if I had a car, I would have left immediately (I suspect my wife knows me too well and this is why she abandoned me with no transportation).

Since I could not flee, I ventured into battle.

First of all, I immediately learned that if you are a somewhat average size, you cannot show up at a big sale at 2:00 p.m. To find deals, you must be there when the doors open. If I were several inches shorter, there were still lots of great pants to choose from. But at this point the 34/34s were nowhere to be found. After 45 minutes, I ended up with five new shirts, but only two were on sale. So much for my grandiose plan.

However, during my shopping spree, I did run into five people I knew. I was able to have some quick conversations and catch up. I even set up lunch with one important person, with whom I had lost touch. You never know when you can do a little business networking.

I then decided to venture out into the open waters of the mall. Again, I glanced at the coffee bar, more in need of caffeine than I had been an hour earlier, and yes, the line was even longer.

The mall was crazy. There were more people than at a rock concert, and it did not take a genius to realize that by December 26, people's Christmas Spirit was already running on empty. The next two hours were peppered with running into more friends and business contacts, who also had decided to brave the After-Christmas sales. Everyone was glad to see a friendly face. I think the chance to take a fast break from the madness of the shopping experience to talk with an acquaintance made their day, too.

Remember, you can network anywhere and everywhere.

# 41 Things
# I've Learned By 40

June 8, 2006 was my 40th Birthday. Here are 41 things I learned along the way:

41. Don't worry too much about what others think about you.

40. Everyone has an ego. Tread lightly so as to not bruise them.

39. Nothing produces results as much as taking action.

38. Don't gossip. What you say will always find its way back to the person you spoke of.

37. People do business with people they know and like.

36. Jealous and petty people are just part of life.

35. Say "please" and "thank you." It will make you stand out from the crowd.

34. When you need help, ask.

33. Written goals are an important step in achieving your dreams.

32. Over using credit cards will stall your financial future.

31. A supportive spouse is worth his or her weight in gold, and then some.

30. A true friend is excited for you about any event that makes you happy.

29. True friends are rare and should be cherished.

28. No job is secure. Have a Plan B.

27. Look for the best in other people. Do not focus on their flaws.

26. You are not what you drive or what you wear. Do not judge others by their cars, clothes or zip code.

25. You are a "brand". No matter what you do, it affects your reputation.

24. Luck does not happen by accident.

23. Start saving money when you are young.

22. Dedicate time to think about your future. Know what success looks like.

21. You cannot love your kids too much!

20. Treat everyone with respect. You never know when they might circle back into your life.

19. If you are not knowledgeable about wine, don't fake it.

18. Befriend your competitors.

17. Regardless of your political beliefs – attend a presidential inauguration once in your lifetime. The whole thing is very cool.

16. Find a mentor.

15. Be a mentor.

14. Staying physically fit gets harder as you get older. But do it anyway.

13. You do not have to be smart to be successful. Tenacity trumps intelligence.

12. Having a strong network of professional contacts is the best career safety net.

11. Read books, magazines, websites, blogs and newspapers. Knowledge is power.

10. Writing a book is hard work. Promoting a book is harder work.

9. Develop your public speaking skills. Join a Toastmasters group and participate actively for two years.

8. There is no substitute for integrity.

7. Have friends who challenge you to be a better person.

6. If you know someone who wrote a book, read it. The biggest compliment you can give an author is to read what they wrote.

5. Helping others always comes back to benefit you.

4. Find a good lawyer, accountant and banker before you need them.

3. Learn to cook.

2.  Opportunities exist. You just have to look
    for them.

and the number one thing I have learned:

1.  Those who have achieved *real* success in life,
    be it financially, emotionally or spiritually, will
    never criticize your dreams and aspirations.
    Instead they will look for ways to share their
    own experiences to help lift you up to higher
    levels. Successful people are rarely jealous and
    welcome the achievements of others.

As with all free advice remember that you get what you
pay for.

# Selling out of Town

If your sales territory takes you beyond the town where you live, you will have challenges in developing a network that can and will refer business. Many people are skeptical of out-of-towners, and no matter how good your intentions, you may be seen as a carpet-bagger.

The first thing you need to do when calling into a new community is to realize that everyone would prefer to do business with those who live in their city. But you can't live everywhere, so you just have to get past that obstacle.

Accept that it will take longer to build real relationships outside of your local geography. You do not have the luxury of running into key contacts at lunch, the mall, church, etc. You have to be committed to showing your face in their city on a regular basis. Even though you cannot visit with everyone every time, you need to let your contacts know that you are there often.

Here are a few ideas that will help:

1. Host a lunch, happy hour or dinner with a group of key folks in your satellite city when you come to town. Invite an eclectic group of people who will

make beneficial contacts for each other; they will remember that you are the catalyst that brings them together.

2. Put together a periodic email newsletter that is full of useful information on your industry. Customize some of it to the specific city you are covering.

3. Ask your existing clients for introductions, referrals or just random ideas. If you do a good job meeting their needs, they will be happy to tell others about you, your product or your service. Let them know what problems you have because you live out of town, and they will want to make their city more hospitable to your needs.

4. Praise their city. Just because you do not choose to live there and prefer the city you already live in does not mean you cannot vocalize the wonderful parts of their town. Remember, they do live there and appreciate that you see the city as a great place, not just a city to sell into.

Finally, patience is key. It takes a long time to build relationships remotely; you just have to stick with it and know that one day you will be accepted in the local business community. Hang in there!

# Starbucks Nation

One of the best things that has come along for casual networking meetings is the proliferation of Starbucks. They are everywhere. They are casual. They are inexpensive compared to the price of a full meal. And most importantly, they are comfortably familiar.

Find a coffee house en route to your office. Make it a habit to leave your house 45 minutes earlier, several times a week. On two of those days schedule a coffee meeting with someone in your network. On the other day or two just go there to read the paper or the latest business book.

Over time you will be amazed how many familiar faces from your business community you will see on a regular basis. This gives you a great and unassuming chance to say hello and keep in touch. Part of building a network is remaining visible and having regular chances to keep in touch. Keeping in touch can take as little effort as a polite "hello" while standing in line for your java.

When you are having meetings, there some days, and sitting alone other days, you will become approachable. If you always have meetings or are always alone, people might not want to disturb you, but since you mix it up, you will not be seen as stuck in a routine or too busy in a meeting. You never know whom you might meet.

# Networking Quotient

Networking is not easy to quantify. The word means so many different things to different people, and the results of your networking efforts can be many years in the making. In addition, it is hard to know exactly how savvy your networking skills are since the results are measured in years, not months.

For these reasons I created The Networking Quotient Quiz. This online assessment tool is designed to make you think about how you react in a variety of networking situations. The 30-question quiz takes about eight minutes to complete, and will instantly show you your personalized "networking quotient" and compare your results to those with similar demographics who have taken the quiz.

Why is this important? Many people do not ever give any serious thought to how they network. Small adjustments in your networking skills, things like your first impression and your follow up, can lead to better opportunities in the future. Often people reach a point where they notice that those who have spent years cultivating business relationships have greater success. By starting today, you can be that person.

Log on today at www.networkingquotient.com and take the quiz. It is fast and free.

# About the Author

Thom Singer has nearly two decades of marketing and business development experience with firms such as RR Donnelley, Brobeck Phleger & Harrison LLP, Andrews Kurth LLP, Marsh, Inc., and Wells Fargo Bank. He is an expert in branding, positioning and networking, and has trained more than 2,000 professionals in the art of building professional contacts that lead to increased business.

Thom has authored numerous articles for business and marketing publications, including The Austin Business Journal, The Legal Marketing Portal and Professional Marketers Forum Magazine . An accomplished speaker and presenter, Thom was a semi-finalist in the 2002 Toastmasters International World Championship of Public Speaking, placing second in the Region III competition, making him among the top 20 Toastmasters of 20,000 who competed that year. He is also the creator of the online networking skills assessment tool, The Networking Quotient ( www.networkingquotient.com )

Thom and his wife, Sara, make their home in Austin, Texas and are the parents of two daughters.

He can be emailed at thom@thomsinger.com.

# Order Form

**Fax orders:** Fax this form to 425-984-7256.
**Telephone orders:** Call 925-838-9806. *Please have your credit card ready.*
**Email orders:** orders@newyearpublishing.com
**Postal orders by credit card or personal check:** *New Year Publishing, LLC*
*PO Box 12793*
*Austin, TX 78711 USA*

**I would like additional information on:** ___Speaking ___Seminars ___Consulting

Name: _____

Address: _____

City: _____State:_____ Zip: _____

Telephone: _____

Email: _____

_____ Quantity @ $29.95 for two books: Some Assembly Required
and The ABC's of Networking
_____ Quantity @ $12.95 for The ABC's of Networking

**Sales tax:** Please add 8.25% for books shipped to California.
**Shipping:** $5.95 per order

_____ Total including applicable tax and shipping

**Payment:** ___Check ___Credit card
Card number: _____
Name on card:_____
Exp. date: _____